Scholastic Young Classics

The Crow and the Eagle

A tale from Aesop's Fables

This book belongs to

____

Published by Scholastic India Pvt. Ltd.
A subsidiary of Scholastic Inc., New York, 10012 (USA).
Publishers since 1920, with international operations in Canada, Australia, New Zealand, the United Kingdom, Mexico, India, Argentina, and Hong Kong.

For information regarding permission, write to:
Scholastic India Pvt. Ltd.
A-27, Ground Floor, Bharti Sigma Centre,
Infocity-I, Sector-34, Gurgaon 122001

Typeset at Digital Expressions

First edition: June 2006
Reprint: July 2012; January; October 2014; July 2015;
September; December 2016; February 2017, 2018, 2019, 2020, 2023, 2024,
February 2026

ISBN: 978-81-7655-461-9

Printed at Shivam Offset Press, New Delhi

The Crow and the Eagle

Rohini Chowdhury

Illustrations
Taposhi Ghoshal

SCHOLASTIC
New York Toronto London Auckland
New Delhi Hong Kong

It was a bright spring day. The sun was high in the blue sky. A herd of sheep was grazing contentedly on the hillside. The little lambs with their soft white coats and curly tails were playing among themselves.

The Shepherd, seeing that his flock was safe and happy, had fallen asleep under the spreading branches of a large old tree.

Suddenly an Eagle swooped down from the sky. It pounced on a little lamb and carried it off so swiftly that none of the other lambs even had the time to bleat. The sleeping Shepherd heard nothing.

A Crow was sitting on the tree under which the Shepherd lay asleep. He had seen how the Eagle had caught the lamb and carried it off to his nest.

'What a wonderful way to get dinner!' he thought. 'Why do crows look for old smelly food?'

The Crow decided to do exactly as the Eagle had done. It had looked easy enough. All he had to do was decide which sheep he wanted, swoop down upon it, hold it as firmly as he could in his claws, and fly off with it. Easy! If the Eagle could do it, then so could he!

The Crow looked down at the flock of sheep to decide which sheep he wanted.

Just below the tree, by the Shepherd, a big, old Ram was grazing. He had curling horns and a thick heavy fleece.

'Aha! He should be a good meal for me!' thought the Crow greedily. He was very hungry, and the thought of a large juicy ram for lunch made his mouth water.

The Crow swooped silently and swiftly down onto the Ram, just as he had seen the Eagle do, and grasped it firmly by its fleece.

'And now to fly off with it to my nest,' said the Crow to himself. He flapped his wings with all his strength, but could not lift the Ram.

The Ram was large. He was much too heavy for the Crow to carry.

The Crow tried again and again, but without success.

The Ram felt the Crow on its back, and was most annoyed. 'Just what do you think you are doing, you pesky bird?' he snapped, glaring at him over his shoulder.

The Crow flapped harder still, trying to carry the Ram away.

'Now stop that!' cried the Ram. 'Go away! Shoo! Leave me in peace!' He jumped and bucked and tried to shake the Crow off his back.

'Oh oh!' thought the Crow, alarmed at the Ram's fierce antics. 'Maybe this wasn't such a good idea after all! Perhaps I should look for my dinner somewhere else! I had better let the Ram be!'

The Crow tried to fly away, but he found he could not move. His claws were caught in the Ram's thick fleece!

The Crow pulled his feet this way and that. He flapped his wings as hard as he could. But no matter what he did, he only seemed to get stuck more firmly.

Oh, how was he ever going to get free? The Crow squawked loudly in fear and despair.

The Ram started running around the tree, bellowing with rage.

The Shepherd woke up with a start. Who was making that horrible noise? Were his sheep in danger? He sat up.

What a sight met his eyes!

The Ram was running round and round the tree. On his back was the Crow, squawking and trying to rise into the air.

The Shepherd began to laugh.

At last, wiping his eyes, the Shepherd stood up. He stopped the Ram as he ran by and calmed him with gentle words.

When the Ram was still, the Shepherd took a pair of shears from his sack. Holding the Crow with one hand, he deftly snipped the fleece until the Crow was free.

'What did you think you were doing, my fine friend?' asked the Shepherd, looking at the Crow. 'Playing at being an Eagle, were you?' The Shepherd burst out laughing again.

The Crow was too embarrassed even to croak. He wished only that the Shepherd would let him go so he could fly away to his nest and hide his foolish head.

Finally, when the Shepherd let the Crow go, the Crow flapped his wings and flew off as fast as he could.

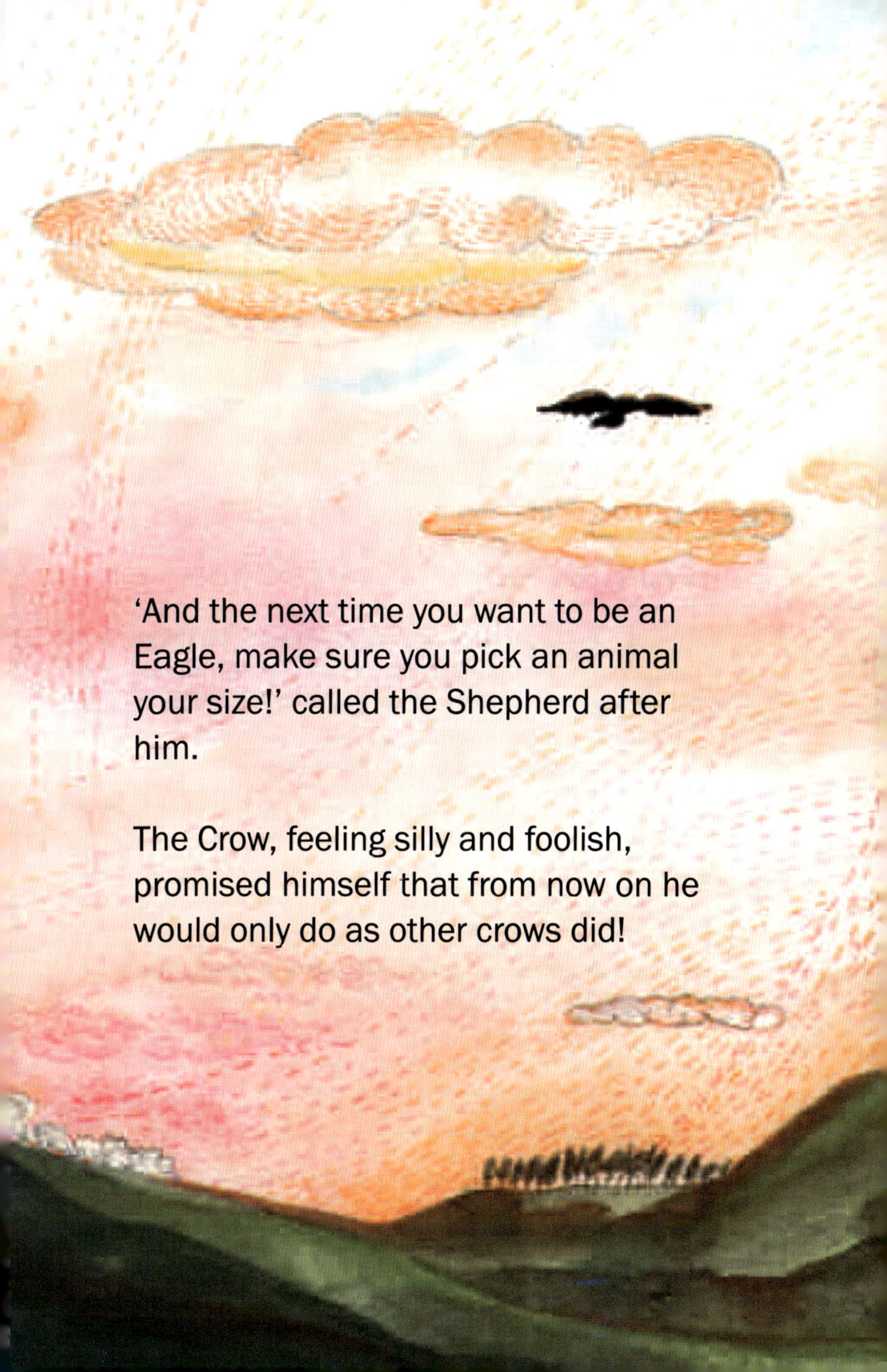

'And the next time you want to be an Eagle, make sure you pick an animal your size!' called the Shepherd after him.

The Crow, feeling silly and foolish, promised himself that from now on he would only do as other crows did!

Note for Parents and Teachers

Parents lay the foundation for their child's success as a reader by reading to him/her. The more books you read to your child, the larger his/her vocabulary will become. A bigger vocabulary will make it possible for him/her to recognise words when he/she reads. This makes the whole process of reading easier. If your child is successful in early attempts to read, he/she will automatically enjoy the process of reading.

You should read aloud to your child at least once every day. Create a special reading time during the day when you can settle down and enjoy a book, without interruption. For many families, reading aloud is a bedtime tradition. The child looks forward to the time spent with the parent, and reading, being associated with that time, becomes something to look forward to.

Not all children take to reading quickly, and it can be quite discouraging to read to a child who does not seem interested. But if you would like your child to become a proficient and happy reader, you must not give up. The more you read to a child and share the pictures the more the child will come to enjoy the whole process. Gradually, your enthusiasm and interest will communicate itself to the child, and the child will learn to listen and to look at the pictures and words on the page. From that to actual reading is a short and exciting step.

Once your child is entranced by the magic of books,

he/she will remain a reader forever.

Even after your child begins to read on his/her own, it is important that you sit and share the experience of reading with him/her. Help if the child gets stuck on any word, explain meanings, and give liberal praise for any successful effort. Children like telling stories as much as they like listening to them, so when your child reads out to you, listen!

Teachers have long recognised that the way to improve students' spelling, vocabulary, reading and writing skills, is directly connected to how often they read or are read to.

Discuss the book with your child after reading. This may be a simple discussion of what happened in the story, or a more complex discussion of how the story relates to experiences the child has had. Sharing of ideas with your child establishes valuable communication habits. Reading about different people and situations increases the child's awareness of the world, and expands his/her understanding.

Read with your child and set him/her off on a voyage of discovery that will last a lifetime!

Reading the Scholastic Young Classics

Scholastic Young Classics is a series of readers, retold from well-known classics, which are designed to give young children a confident and successful start to reading.

These books are designed to be read aloud to younger children who are beginning to read. They are also suitable for reading by children who are familiar with simple words and can read short sentences by themselves.

Each story contains

- Simple sentences and words
- Clear type
- Memorable characters
- Frequent repetition of phrases, which helps the child to read fluently
- Vivid and detailed illustrations, which correspond closely to the text, but add new dimensions to it. This enables children to understand the text, and at the same time, provides the child with interesting visual details that enliven and enhance the written word.

About the Author

Rohini Chowdhury has written several books for children, including *The Three Princes of Persia* and *White Tiger*. She runs a story website for children at www. longlongtimeago.com.
Rohini lives in London with her husband and two daughters.

About the Illustrator

Taposhi Ghoshal, a graduate of the College of Art, New Delhi, received the Kalatrayee Award from the Director of Education in 1985. As a freelance illustrator and designer, she has worked with several publishing houses and NGOs, including KATHA, Pratham books, Actionaid, Care India, Penguin India, Ladybird, NBT and Ratna Sagar.